Irresistible
A,B,Cs

by Joan Novelli

SCHOLASTIC
PROFESSIONAL BOOKS

NEW YORK • TORONTO • LONDON • AUCKLAND • SYDNEY
MEXICO CITY • NEW DELHI • HONG KONG

For my favorite young readers,
Dylan, Elena, Sara, and Jonathan

Special thanks to the talented teachers who contributed ideas to this book:
Peg Arcadi, Denise Dauler, Janet Fuller, Jim Henry, Monica Lubic,
Elaine Magud, Carol McQuillen, Mary Rosenberg, Charlotte Sassman,
Mary Beth Spann, and Natalie Vaughan.

Cover design by Norma Ortiz
Cover art by John Wallace
Interior design by Solutions by Design, Inc.
Interior art by Liisa Chauncy Guida, except pages 29–31 by Rusty Fletcher, pages 32 and 43 by Abby Carter, and page 11 by James Graham Hale

"Eat the Alphabet" by Meish Goldish from *Thematic Songs, Poems and Fingerplays* by Meish Goldish.
Copyright © 1993 by Scholastic Inc.

ISBN 0-590-04930-5

Contents

About This Book

♪♪♪ A, B, C, D, E, F, G…can you hear it? The alphabet song is one of those melodies that seems to stay with us forever. Maybe that's because learning the alphabet song as a youngster is full of promise. These are the letters that will unlock the magic of reading. Children seem to acquire the song a few letters at a time—with each new addition bringing immeasureable delight and pride. They progress from being able to say and sing the alphabet to being able to recognize printed forms of the letters. Recognizing letters with accuracy and speed gives children the mental energy they need to learn the sound-spelling relationships that lead to fluent reading and writing.

This book is designed to help you guide children in this exciting process. Many of the activities come from classroom teachers across the country. All of the activities will support and enrich your literacy program, whatever your approach. Highlights include:

✸ **Multisensory Activities:** Your students will engage their senses with activities that invite them to listen, touch, see, and say. Kinesthetic activities let them learn through movement.

✸ **Reproducible Activity Pages:** Use these games, templates, poems, and more to support learning.

✸ **Building on Books:** Enhance learning with picture books that reinforce alphabet recognition and sound-letter associations. See Building on Books throughout for suggested titles and follow-up activities.

✸ **Poetry and Songs:** A rhyming ABC poem and fun fingerplay invite lots of literacy spinoffs.

✸ **Interactive Displays:** Pocket chart activities, word walls, banners, and other displays invite children to collaborate in the learning process.

✸ **Computer Connections:** Learn how you can enhance your literacy program with award-winning software, teacher-tested web sites, and other technology tools.

✸ **Where to Learn More:** Find out about teacher resources for building a rich literacy program.

✸ **And Lots More!**

Learning about letters—the way they look, the sounds they represent, and the meaning they make as words—can be filled with fun. When it is, children carry that joy of learning beyond the classroom, using what they learn to grow as lifelong writers and readers.

TIP

When planning literacy activities, try to build in several levels of difficulty so that each child can experience success. Share *The Three Bears* with children and talk about finding a task that is "not too easy, not too hard, but just right." Walk students through a literacy activity to show them the different ways they can approach it. For example, if students are sorting letters on a T-chart (see page 9), some might simply sort, some might sort and say the letters, others might sort and say the letters and their sounds.

Elaine Magud
Joshua Cowell School
Manteca, California

Letters Lead the Way

Lots of Letters

Encourage early literacy skills by stocking your classroom with a variety of letter manipulatives. Aim for assorted sizes, shapes, and colors. Suggestions follow.

* **Sign-Making Letters:** A signmaker or hardware store might be willing to donate letters for making signs.

* **Sandpaper Letters:** Cut block letters out of sandpaper or purchase them.

* **Alphabet Magnets:** An old refrigerator door (check with a local appliance store) bolted safely to a wall makes a great place to play with letter magnets. Cookie sheets are a fun place to play with magnetic letters, too.

* **Printer Letters:** Print out letters of the alphabet in different fonts, using an extra large type size (such as 72). Laminate and cut apart letters.

* **Alphabet Stamps:** Provide ink in assorted colors and 1-inch graph paper (see page 45) for stamping letters of the alphabet in sequence, names, and so on.

* **Alphabet Blocks:** Gather scrap wood from a lumber store and let children make alphabet blocks. The pieces do not have to be cubes but it is helpful to have them be fairly uniform in size (such as a 2-by-4 cut into 4-inch wide pieces). Let children use acrylic paints to write the letters of the alphabet on the wood, one letter per piece. Paint on a base coat first, if desired. Let dry before children paint on letters.

> Monica Lubic
> Charlotte Central School
> Charlotte, Vermont

What's the best order in which to teach the letters of the alphabet? Many children come to school knowing the traditional ABC song, and you may want to teach the letters in the same order. Or, you may teach the letters that are most closely related to the sounds they make. In *Phonics From A to Z* (Scholastic Professional Books, 1998), Wiley Blevins explains that "21 letters contain the most common sound assigned to them in their names—for example, *b* (/be/) and *m* (/em/). The exceptions are *h*, *q*, *w*, *y*, *g*, and the short vowels."

Some teachers prefer to teach the letters in children's names, as these letters have special meaning to them. Another consideration to keep in mind is that some letters, such as *b* and *d*, are visually confusing to many children. It may be best to space these letters in your program so that children can learn one before being introduced to the other.

Letters for Lunch

Share the poem "Eat the Alphabet" with children. (See page 16.) Ask: *Which of these foods would make a good lunch?* Write a class version of the poem called "Letters for Lunch," letting children substitute lunch foods (healthy, silly, or otherwise) for each letter of the alphabet. To begin, copy the poem on chart paper, leaving blanks for each food. Let children suggest foods for each letter of the alphabet, telling a little something extra to complete the second line of each verse. Read the new poem together. Make a pocket chart version for children to play with on their own. Copy each line on a sentence strip, leaving blanks for each food. Write the words for the foods on sentence strips and trim. Children can read the poem, inserting the cards that complete each line.

BUILDING ON BOOKS

Eating the Alphabet
by Lois Ehlert
(Harcourt Brace, 1989)

Luscious watercolors bring fruits and vegetables to life in this colorful book. Plan an alphabet snack in honor of a target letter. How about blueberries, bananas, and bialies for the letter *B*? (For a related activity, see Letters for Lunch, left.)

A is __apple__ , B is __bluecheese__,
C is __crepes if you please__ ,
D is _____ , E is _____ ,
F is _____ .

Where to Learn More

For more alphabet poems and songs, try these wonderful resources.

AlphaTales (Scholastic Professional Books, 2000). Build phonemic awareness and alphabet recognition skills with 26 storybooks—one for each letter of the alphabet.

Animal Poems From A to Z by Meish Goldish (Scholastic Professional Books, 1994). Poems for each letter of the alphabet plus related activities reinforce a range of reading skills.

Sing Along and Learn: The Alphabet by Ken Sheldon (Scholastic Professional Books, 1999). This audiocassette/book set features easy songs to sing and activities to help children master letter sounds, build phonemic awareness, and more.

TIP

As an extension to Letters for Lunch, let children illustrate each food and write the corresponding letter on a paper plate. Place the paper plates at a table. Children can visit independently or in small groups, "setting the table" while saying the names of the letters and the foods. Move the plates to a large space and let children line them up alphabetically.

It's Our Alphabet!

Start the year by having children create alphabet picture cards, one for each letter of the alphabet. Display them in a prominent place in the classroom, within easy eyesight of children. Children respond to this handmade literacy tool in a special way. Having created the cards themselves, they feel an ownership of the letters in the alphabet. As they learn about letters—their shapes, the sounds they stand for, and the words they can make—children will turn to these picture cards often and with great pride.

Carol McQuillen
Orchard School
South Burlington, Vermont

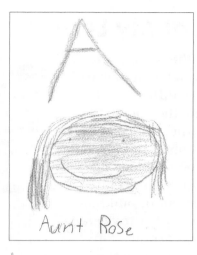

Aunt Rose

Move and Match

Reinforce letter recognition with an alphabet game. Copy pages 17 and 18. Cut apart the cards and punch a hole in the top left and right corners. String with yarn to make necklaces. Give each child a necklace. Make sure for every uppercase letter you hand out, you give someone the matching lowercase letter. (Depending on how many students you have, you may not use each letter. Or, you may invite a neighboring class to join in.) Have children move about the room, looking for the child who has a matching letter. When children find their letter matches, have them sit down together. When all children have found their partners, invite each pair to stand up together and say their letter. Some might also add a word that starts with that letter.

A Silly Alphabet Song

Many primary classes begin the year reviewing or learning the alphabet song for the first time. You can expand on this with Frances the Badger's help. Read the book, *Bedtime For Frances* by Russell Hoban (HarperCollins, 1960). In it, Frances sings a very silly alphabet song that she composes as she goes along. (Children universally howl when Frances sings, "T is for tiger, U is for underwear down in the drier.") Using the rhythm of Frances' song, have students create short phrases or sentences that feature a word that begins with the target letter. Put these together and create your own silly alphabet song.

Bob Krech
Dutch Neck School
Princeton Junction, New Jersey

....

Use the necklaces for more alphabet fun.

✿ Using only the uppercase or the lowercase set of letters, give each child a necklace. Have children arrange themselves in ABC order. This is a fun way to line up for lunch or special activities, too.

✿ Place 26 push pins in a bulletin board strip. Let children arrange the letters alphabetically, hanging them on the push pins.

✿ Let children arrange themselves to spell words. These can be words they know or words they see around the room.

Look at My Letters!

"Look at the *K* we made!" As children begin to learn the shapes different letters make, they begin to discover the shapes in the toys they play with, even in themselves! Snap pictures of the letters children form out of building blocks and other toys and themselves arranged in letter formation on the

floor. When you've got pictures of all the letters, enlarge them and put your special alphabet on display. Later, you can put the pages together to make a book. Children will enjoy borrowing it to share with their families.

> Charlotte Sassman
> Alice Carlson Applied Learning Center
> Fort Worth, Texas

Your Name and Mine

Reinforce letter recognition by letting children look for letters in their names that they have in common. Start by having children print their names in big letters at the top of a piece of paper. Have them draw a thick line across the paper about two-thirds of the way down. Let children mingle, comparing their names to see if they have letters in common. If they have at least one letter in common with someone, have them add their names to the top section of the paper and circle the letters that are the same. If they have no letters in common, have them write their names below the line. When students finish comparing their names, let them share their results. Guide them by asking questions, such as:

☀ Did more children have some letters in common with you or no letters in common with you?

☀ Who had the most letters in common with you?

> Denise Dauler
> El Carmelo School
> Palo Alto, California

BUILDING ON BOOKS

Chicka Chicka Boom Boom
by Bill Martin Jr.
and John Archambault
(Simon & Schuster, 1989)

Let children explore this alphabet story on their own with magnetic letters and a cookie sheet version of the famous coconut tree. Paint a coconut tree on a cookie sheet. (Check to make sure the sheet will hold magnetic letters—some will not.) Use acrylic paint and several layers of varnish for durability. Place the cookie sheet, letters, and a copy of the book at a center. Let students recreate the story, placing the magnetic letters in the tree.

> Elaine Magud
> Joshua Cowell School
> Manteca, California

To reinforce letter recognition at home, have children and families look for particular letters in books they read. You can send home books and response journals and request that they find and write down words in the book that start with the letter of focus—for example, the same letters as their first or last names.

Show What You Know T-Chart

Make a T-chart for learning more about letters. Set up the T-chart on chart paper. Laminate for durability. Label a sorting rule on each side of the chart—for example, Letters

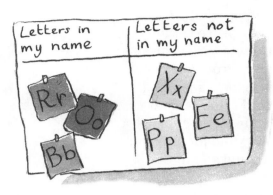

in My Name, Letters Not in My Name. Provide letters for children to sort. (You can print them out on the computer, using large type size and fun fonts.) Other sorting rules you might try include:

☀ Letters That Have Curves, Letters That Are All Straight

☀ Letters in the Name of Our Town, Letters Not in the Name of Our Town

☀ Letters That Are Vowels, Letters That Are Not Vowels

Children can work at three levels on this activity: sorting only; sorting letters and saying them; and sorting them, saying them, and saying the sounds they make.

Elaine Magud
Joshua Cowell School
Manteca, California

Rainbow Letters

Print a letter (make it big) in uppercase and lowercase form on a sheet of paper for each child. (This may be a target letter for the week, the first letter of a child's first name, and so on.) Have children trace around the letters several times using different color crayons. Let children share their rainbow letters with the class, tracing the shape with their fingers and saying the letter. Keep each child's rainbow letters together in a folder. Let children arrange the letters in alphabetical order from time to time. When they have all the letters of the alphabet (or letters that spell their name), bind the pages to make books.

Natalie Vaughan
Phoenix School
Encinitas, California

Check discount stores for inexpensive letter tiles. Children can use them for the T-chart activities.

BUILDING ON BOOKS

26 Letters and 99 Cents

by Tana Hoban
(Scholastic, 1987)

Start on one side of this book, and you get 26 glossy, colorful letters, photographed with everyday objects. Turn the book around, and you've got the same thing with numbers. Use the simple layout and use of everyday objects to inspire a class alphabet display. Have children form letters out of clay, school glue (squeezed into the shapes of letters on paper), or string (shaped and glued on paper). Then have them find objects in the classroom for each letter. Arrange letters and objects on a table. Invite other members of your school community to visit your display.

Sorting Station

Start the school year with a multi-level activity that strengthens young children's concepts of print. To set up the activity, divide a piece of poster board into three parts. Label the first one Picture and glue a picture from a magazine in that section. Label the next Letter (glue a sampling of individual letters here) and the last Word (glue several words here). Gather an assortment of pictures and glue to index cards cut in half or quarters. You may find pictures in magazines, in clip art computer programs, and so on. Cut index cards in quarters and write a letter on each. These might be letters generated on your computer, cut out of magazines and newspapers, clipped from packaging materials (such as cereal boxes), and so on. Cut another set of index cards in quarters and write a word on each (or cut from magazines, print on the computer, and so on). You may wish to laminate picture, letter, and word cards for durability. Place pictures, letters, and words in a box or envelope. Model how to use the board and picture/letter/word cards for the following activities. Remind children to choose the activity that feels right for them.

☀ Sort pictures, letters, and words into appropriate columns, using the graphics on the board as clues.

☀ Sort pictures, letters, and words. Say the letters as you sort them.

☀ Sort pictures, letters, and words. Say each letter and try to find a picture and word that has the same beginning sound.

☀ Sort pictures, letters, and words. Say each letter and try to find a picture and word that has the same beginning sound. Read the words.

Elaine Magud
Joshua Cowell School
Manteca, California

COMPUTER CONNECTION

You can find great pictures, letters, and labels to download at this Reading Recovery site:

www.amihome.com/ rrca/rrcalabels.htm

BUILDING ON BOOKS

Dr. Seuss's ABC

by Dr. Seuss
(Random House, 1963)

"Big A, little a
What begins with A?
Aunt Annie's
alligator........A..a..A"

Each letter has a verse that's just as much fun as this one. Sing the story to the tune of the alphabet song. Reread it often, letting children substitute their own words for each letter.

Letter-Building Interactive Display

This bulletin board invites children to play with the shapes that form letters. Start by covering a bulletin board with craft paper. Cut large shapes from tagboard that represent the basic shapes in letters. Punch holes as shown. (See below.) Make multiple copies of each shape and tack them up to the board along with a box of brads. Let children visit the display in groups of two or three and use the brads to join the shapes and form letters. Have children return the shapes to the board when they are finished.

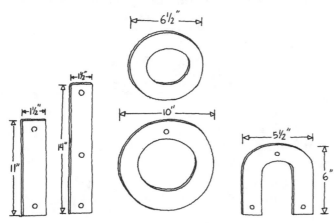

Where to Learn More

For more literacy-building displays, see *Interactive Bulletin Boards: Language Arts* by Joan Novelli and Judy Meagher (Scholastic Professional Books, 1998).

I'm on the Phone!

Add play phones (or recycled phones) and phone books to a dramatic play area. Young children like to pretend to look up numbers at random and make calls. Eventually, they become interested in finding their own names and numbers in the phone book, as well as the same information for friends, a favorite pizza shop, a toy store, and so on.

Monica Lubic
Charlotte Central School
Charlotte, Vermont

Letter Line Up

Write each alphabet letter on an index card. Put the cards in a bag. When it's time to line up for lunch or another activity, do it by the first letters of children's names. Start by pulling a random letter out of the bag. Call out the letter and hold up the card. Let children whose first names start with that letter get in line. Continue until all children have lined up. Just for fun reveal the letters that have not been called. How many letters of the alphabet do not correspond to the first letters of children's names? Once children see how it's done, they can take over. Let a volunteer each day pull the letters from the bag one at a time and call them out so children can line up.

Name Sort

Children can revisit this activity often to learn about letters and their classmates' names. Draw 26 squares on a sheet of poster board. Label each square with a letter of the alphabet. Place a picture on each square to represent the sound of the letter—for example, an apple for the letter *a*. (You can use stickers, pictures cut from magazines, or your own drawings.) Print students' names on small cards. Let children sort the names by first letter, placing them on the poster board in the correct squares.

> Elaine Magud
> Joshua Cowell School
> Manteca, California

Letter Bingo

Bingo is always a favorite with children. Use the bingo board on page 19 to reinforce letter recognition. Start by giving each child a blank Bingo board. Have children print a letter of the alphabet in each square. The letters do not need to be in any order. Students will use all but two letters of the alphabet. Make a set of letter cards (copy pages 17–18 or just write the letters on slips of paper). Put

BUILDING ON BOOKS

Farm Alphabet Book
by Jane Miller
(Scholastic, 1981)

Students will enjoy predicting what part of a farm the author pictures for each letter of the alphabet. Make an alphabet book about the area where your students live. Let each child illustrate a page.

For more name-sorting fun, look around for an old Rolodex or similar system. Have children write their names (first and last) on blank cards. Have them file their names alphabetically by first or last names. Take out the cards each day so that children can revisit the activity.

the letters in a box or bag. Give each child a set of Bingo markers (dried beans will work) and you're ready to play.

❋ Start by having children place a marker on the free space.

❋ Pull a letter out of the bag. Show students the letter and invite them to say it with you. If students have this letter on their boards, have them place a marker on it.

❋ Continue until a student has filled up a row—horizontally, vertically, or diagonally.

❋ Continue playing to see how many students can fill up one or more rows.

Letter Art

Gather twigs, leaves, cotton balls, and other assorted materials (all safe to touch). Let children use them to form the letters of their names. When they've settled on an arrangement, they can glue the letters in place on tagboard. These multisensory nameplates are fun to make and rewarding as finished products. They'll look terrific tacked up around the classroom or hung up at home.

ABC Race

Everyone's a winner in a cooperative race that reinforces letter recognition and alphabetical order. Children will have fun playing it again and again to beat the class time.

❋ Prepare for the race by making a set of letter cards.

❋ Gather children in a circle. Mix up the cards and give one to each child. Give children additional cards until you have passed out all of the cards. Explain that you are

going to call out the letters in order, starting with *A*. When children hear their letters, they need to hold up their cards over their heads. Tell students that you are going to time them to see how fast the class can get through all of the letters in order.

☀ Call out the letter *A* and wait for the child with that card to hold it up. Continue calling the letters in order, having each child hold up his or her card in turn. Stop the clock when the child with *Z* holds up that card.

☀ Talk about strategies for improving the class time then have another race. Can students work together to improve their time?

Natalie Vaughan
Phoenix School
Encinitas, California

Edible Letters

Celebrate your students' success with learning the alphabet by making letter cookies. You can use the recipe here, your own favorite recipe, or prepared cookie dough from the grocery store. Let children take turns rolling out the dough and cutting out shapes with letter cookie cutters. Bake, decorate, and enjoy!

Cookie Dough
1 1/4 cups flour
1/3 cup sugar
1/2 cup butter
1 egg
1 teaspoon vanilla

Mix flour, sugar, and butter. Stir in the egg and vanilla. Roll out the dough and cut out the cookies! Bake on a greased cookie sheet for 10 to 15 minutes at 350° F. Frost and add sprinkles if desired.

I Spy Letters! Game

Let children play this letter-matching game in small groups to reinforce letter recognition skills.

☀ Make a copy of the game board on page 20 for each group. Laminate for durability if desired. Give each group two pennies, game markers (such as dried beans) and play!

☀ To play, have children take turns tossing the pennies. If both land on heads, the child moves 1 space. If both land on tails, the child moves 2 spaces. If one lands on heads and the other tails, the child moves three spaces. When children land on a space they need to say the letter, then find the same letter in the print around the room and say "I spy the letter [name letter] [tell place]. For a challenge, children can say the word in which the letter appears if they wish.

Make a copy of the game board for each child to take home. Encourage children to play with their families. They can play again and again, making new matches for the letters they land on.

15

Eat the Alphabet

A is Apple, B is Bean,
C is Celery, fresh and green.

D is Doughnut, E is Egg,
F is Fig, rolling down your leg!

G is Grapefruit, H is Honey,
I is Ice cream, soft and runny.

J is Jello, K is Knish,
L is Lettuce and Lic-o-rice!

M is Meatball, N is Nut,
O is Orange, peeled or cut.

P is Pizza, Q is Quince,
R is Rice fit for a prince!

S is Spaghetti, T is Tangerine,
U is Upside-down cake with cream
between.

V is Vegetable soup, W is Waffle,
X is scrambled X. (Isn't that joke awful!)

Y is Yogurt, Z is Zucchini,
Let's eat the alphabet on a bed of linguine!

—Meish Goldish

"Eat the Alphabet" by Meish Goldish from *Thematic Songs, Poems and Fingerplays* by Meish Goldish. Copyright © 1993 by Scholastic Inc.

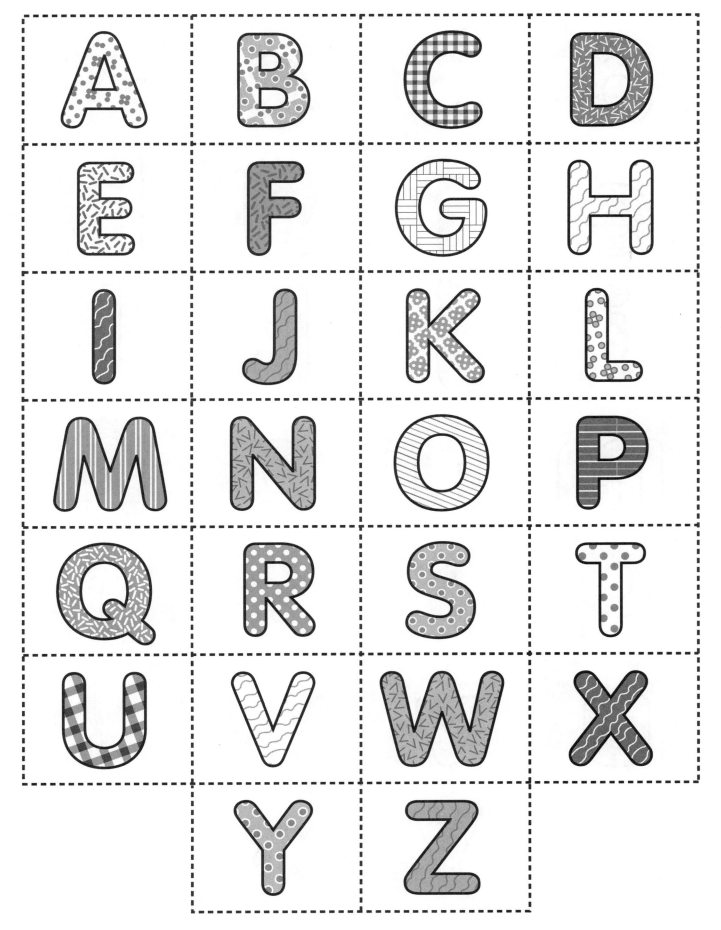

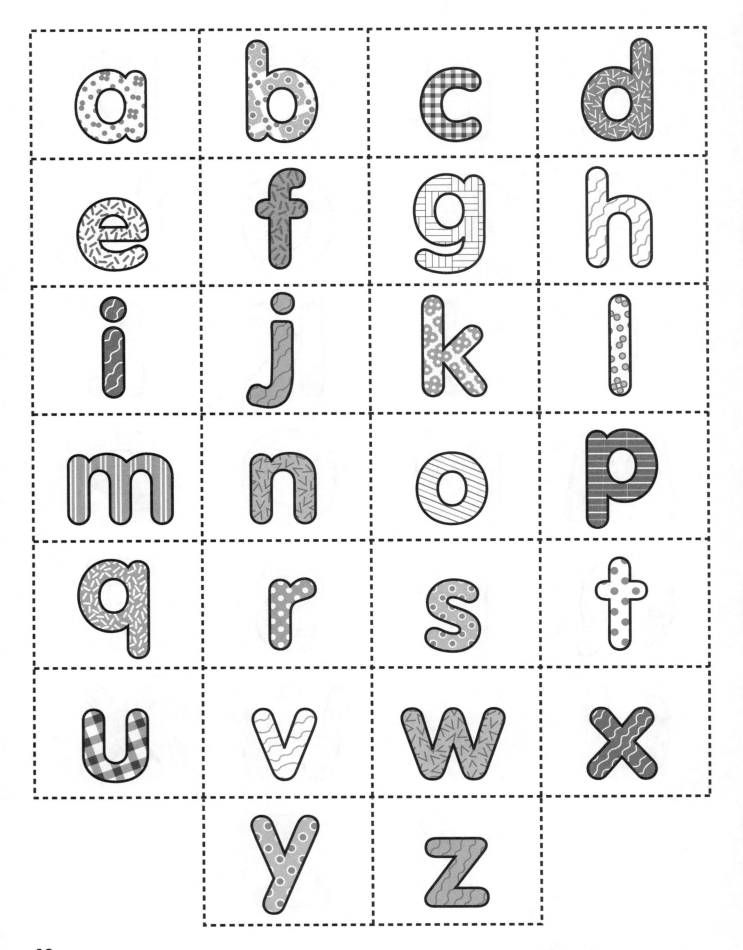

Irresistible ABCs Scholastic Professional Books

Name _____ Date _____

Letter Bingo Board

Name _____ Date _____

I Spy Letters! Game

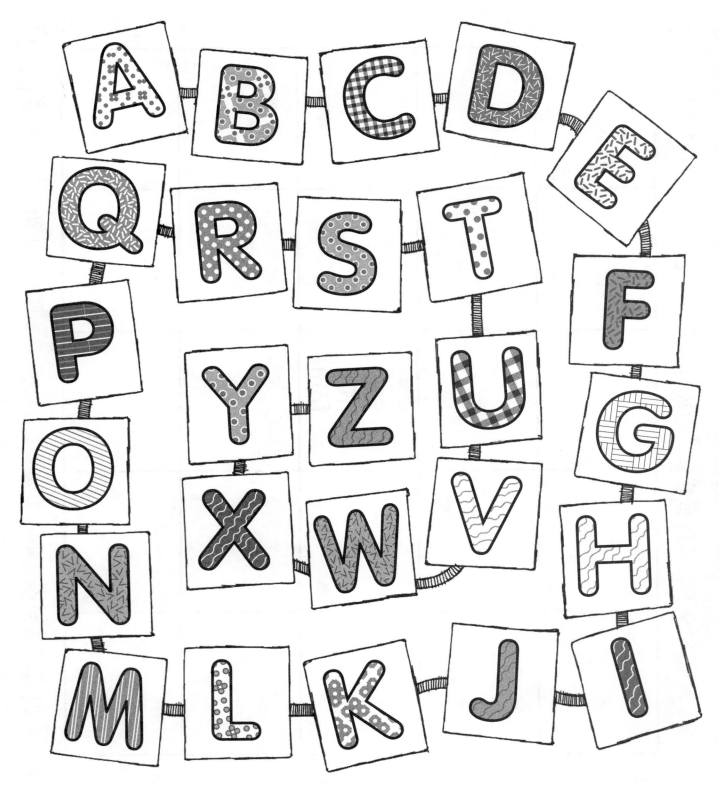

Irresistible ABCs Scholastic Professional Books

Linking Letters and Sounds

Picture Dictionary Mural

Write the alphabet, upper and lower case, on large sheets of craft paper. Place them around the classroom on tables, or in a larger space on the floor. Let children visit the letters, drawing pictures to go with each letter. You may do a few letters a day, so that children have plenty of time with each letter.

Label children's drawings, then display as a mural from clothespins. This mural becomes a picture dictionary for students to use all year. Take the "pages" down every couple of months so that children can revisit the letters and add new pictures and labels.

> Jim Henry
> Lomond Elementary School
> Shaker Heights, Ohio

Where to Learn More

Jim Henry shares more mini-lessons and skill-building strategies in *Fresh Takes on Using Journals to Teach Beginning Writers* (Scholastic Professional Books, 1999).

ABC Circus Train

Reinforce sound-letter associations by creating a colorful, collaborative ABC banner. Start by making a copy of pages 29 (the engine) and 31. Make a class set of page 30. Give each child a copy of page 30. Have children complete the rhyme for an assigned letter. Complete page 31 as a class for the letter *Z*. Have children link the train cars with color-

---

BUILDING ON BOOKS

Clifford's ABC
by Norman Bridwell
(Scholastic, 1983)

Clifford adorns each page of this book, which features a busy picture for each letter of the alphabet. Each item in the picture is labeled, and a list for each letter reinforces the words in alphabetical order. Children will have fun using this book to help choose pictures and words for the Picture Dictionary Mural (above) and the A–Z Pocket Chart. (See page 24.)

ful round stickers. Add the engine and display! To turn students' pages into a book, just fold the banner back and forth accordion-style. Back the banner with sturdy paper first for durability.

Where to Learn More

ABC Circus Train was adapted from *30 Instant Collaborative Classroom Banners* by Deborah Schecter (Scholastic Professional Books, 1999), a collection of easy-to-make banners that celebrates special days, favorite topics, and more.

ABC Word Wall

Introduce letters of the alphabet, build recognition of sound-letter relationships, reinforce phonemic awareness, and more with an ABC word wall. Begin by selecting a word or letter for focus, based on a story, poem, or rhyme you share with children. For example, if you read *A Pair of Protoceratops* by Bernard Most (Harcourt Brace, 1998), you can focus on the letter *p*. Protoceratops in this book paint pictures, paste paper, practice penmanship, plunge into pools, put on pajamas, and more—each time reinforcing the letter *p*.

* After sharing the story, call attention to words in the story that start with the letter *p* (in this case, almost all of them).

* Start your word wall by writing one of these words (such as *protoceratops*) on a card or sentence strip. Have a child make a picture to go with the word.

* Let children find more key words from the book. Write them on word cards and have children illustrate them.

* Revisit the words from day to day, reading them together and having children practice writing them (or just the first letter) on their own paper. Encourage children to see that learning how to write the letter *p* will help them learn to read and write words with this letter.

COMPUTER CONNECTION

Children will have fun using *Kid Pix Deluxe* (Broderbund) to make alphabet books in the style of *From Acorn to Zoo*. They can choose from hundreds of rubber stamps to create pictures for each letter, and add text and their own pictures, too.

BUILDING ON BOOKS

From Acorn to Zoo
by Satoshi Kitamura
(Scholastic, 1992)

"What is the armadillo balancing on his nose?" The armadillo happens to be balancing an apple, apricot, almond, and acorn, in that order. A larger picture above the armadillo shows all these things and more—each of them labeled, each of them a word for *A*. The same format is followed for the other letters, making this busy book one that children can pore over again and again, learning something new each time. Of course, a reading of this book begs to be followed by a new version by your students. Team them up for each letter, or let them work independently.

Where to Learn More

For more great word wall ideas, see *Teaching Reading and Writing With Word Walls* by Janet M. Wagstaff (Scholastic Professional Books, 1999).

In the Bag

Reinforce children's understanding of sound-letter relationships with this take-home activity. Give each child a paper bag on which you've written a target letter. This could be the first letter of the child's first name or some other letter you'd like to focus on. Have children fill their bags with objects that start with the letters on their bags. For example, if Pilar's bag has the letter *p* on it, she might find a pencil, paper, paperclip, playing card, picture book, and so on. Have children bring the bags back to school and share them with the class. You might make an alphabet word wall to record children's findings. Guide students to notice each word's initial letter and sound.

COMPUTER CONNECTION

A to Zap (Sunburst) is full of fun early literacy explorations. A simple set-up makes it easy for young children to navigate the program all by themselves. The program opens to a colorful keyboard, with each key labeled by letter. Children access activities by clicking on the letters. Holding the cursor over a letter results in the letter being pronounced. Clicking on the letter makes several things happen. A word starting with the letter is pronounced, displayed, and spelled. A picture appears as well. Click on the picture and any number of things can happen. For example, click on x and hear/see the word *x-ray*. Click on the picture, and objects (such as an apple, car, and child) will appear. Click on the objects for x-ray views. Click on any letter and see the x-ray view of the object that goes with that letter—a dog, a fish, and so on. Each letter comes with its own surprises, making this a delightful introduction to sound-letter relationships.

BUILDING ON BOOKS

It Begins With an A
by Stephanie Calmenson
(Scholastic, 1993)

"You travel in this. It begins with an A. It starts on the ground then flies up, up, away! What is it?" This book is written in rhymes—one for each letter of the alphabet. It will easily inspire your students to write their own alphabet riddles. You might try some as a class, then let students team up (younger children may work well with older buddies) to make their own. Make a display, or put pages together to make an alphabet book.

TIP

Vary this activity to have children collaborate on filling an ABC box. Make the box by decorating a shoe box with letters of the alphabet and pictures of things that represent those letters. Or, wrap the box in wrapping paper printed with letters. Write a target letter on a piece of paper and tape it to the box. Let children fill the box with objects that represent the target letter. When the box is full, let children take turns selecting an object from the box and naming it. As a bonus, they can try to spell the word.

A–Z Pocket Chart

Build an understanding of sound-letter relationships with this pocket chart activity.

☀ Cut sentence strips into thirds. Write a letter of the alphabet on each card—both upper and lowercase.

☀ Cut another set of sentence strips into thirds. Glue a picture on each card to match (beginning sound) the letters—for example, a picture of apple for the letter *A*. *Clifford's ABC* is full of ideas for picture cards. (See Building on Books, 21.)

☀ Cut a third set of sentence strips into thirds. Write the word for each picture on a card.

☀ Place the letter cards in the pocket chart. Say each letter as you place the card in the pocket chart. Play a game as you take them out. Say each letter, one at a time. Let children take turns finding that letter and taking it out.

☀ Place picture and letter cards in the pocket chart. Let children take turns matching the cards. Encourage them to say the letter and the sound it makes as they make each match.

☀ When your students are ready, add the word cards. Children can match letter and word cards, or all three sets of cards.

☀ Encourage children to make their own picture and word cards to add to the A–Z pocket chart.

Where to Learn More

For more interactive literacy-building pocket chart activities, see *Pocket Charts for Emergent Readers* by Valerie SchifferDanoff (Scholastic Professional Books, 1997).

BUILDING ON BOOKS

A Trio of Triceratops
by Bernard Most
(Harcourt Brace, 1998)

Books with alliteration heighten awareness of letter-sound relationships. *A Trio of Triceratops* has one alliterative line per page, making it easy for children to make the association between the letter *t* and the corresponding sound. ("A trio of triceratops touching their toes.") This book happens to double as a great math lesson. Introduce the word "trio," and ask children if they can guess what it means. Encourage children to notice the way the numbers 1, 2, and 3 pop up now and then in the illustrations. Help them make the connection. For more fun with alliteration and a math lesson on pairs, try *A Pair of Protoceratops*, also by Bernard Most.(See page 22.)

TIP

You may wish to color code the sentence strips, making each set of letter, picture, and word cards a different color.

Looking for Letters

Set up a display to let children discover the many shapes and sizes letters can be. Start by choosing a letter of focus. Let's say you're sharing a rhyme in which a particular letter stands out—for example, the letter *i* in Ten Fingers. (See right.) Write the rhyme on chart paper and display. Read the rhyme with children, having them move their hands as indicated. Then give each child a copy of the rhyme. Let children circle each *i* on their papers. Then have children look for the letter *i* in magazines and newspapers, on packaging and junk mail, and so on. Have children cut out the words and paste them around the display.

AlphaBugs

You can count on bugs to hold children's interest. Combine a unit on bugs with this literacy-building activity. Start by sharing a simple alphabet book such as David McPhail's *Animals* (Scholastic, 1989). This story simply lists animals alphabetically: *A Ant, Armadillo; B Bear, Bird,* and so on. What's helpful is that children will see how they can get creative with difficult letters. For example, *U* is *Unicorn* and *Upside-down catfish*.

Follow up by making a collaborative ABC book about bugs. Each child can choose a letter, or you can work as a class, making sure each child gets to make a contribution. Have children illustrate the pages, conducting simple research if necessary to see what the bugs look like. Students will enjoy reading this book aloud as a class, with each child reading his or her page. See Tip (right) for a list of bugs students might use.

Ten Fingers

I have ten little fingers
And they all belong to me.
I can make them do things.
Would you like to see?
I can shut them up tight
Or open them wide.
I can put them together
Or make them all hide.
I can make them jump high,
I can make them jump low,
I can fold them quietly
And hold them just so.
　　　—Anonymous

TIP

A sampling of bugs from A to Z include:

A antlion
B backswimmer
C click beetle
D dragonfly
E earwig
F firefly
G glow worm
H honeybee
I inchworm
J japyx
K katydid
L leafhopper
M millipede
N night crawler
O oil beetle
P pill bug
Q queen bee
R roly-poly
S scorpion
T tiger beetle
U unicorn caterpillar
V vinegar fly
W whirligig beetle
X xysticus elegans
Y yellow-spotted millipede
Z zerene fritillary

Chants, Rhymes, and Fingerplays

Chants, rhymes, and fingerplays are fun ways to reinforce sound-letter associations. Many of them contain phonograms or word families—such as the letters -*ack* in Miss Mary Mack. (See page 32.) Learning word families is an effective tool for young readers. By knowing the sound a group of letters makes, children can more quickly and efficiently read new words. So, for example, a child who knows the sound the letters -*ack* make can apply that knowledge to read lots of words—*back, Jack, quack, stack*, and so on. They do this by recognizing the sound several letters make together (rather than sounding out and blending individual letters), developing fluency in the process.

Share Miss Mary Mack with children for a hand-clapping rhyme that repeats words in a predictable pattern, reinforcing both the -*ack* phonogram and the sounds that go with beginning letters. To keep interest alive as you repeat rhymes, chants, or fingerplays, try these variations.

☀ Have children clap out the rhyme with partners as they chant or sing it.

☀ Ask children to whisper the rhyme.

☀ Let children shout the rhyme.

☀ Challenge children to say the rhyme slowly.

☀ Have children say the rhyme as fast as they can.

Janet Fuller
The Children's School
South Burlington, Vermont

BUILDING ON BOOKS

On Market Street
by Arnold Lobel
(Scholastic, 1981)

"The merchants down on Market Street were opening their doors. I stepped along that Market Street, I stopped at all the stores. Such wonders there on Market Street! So much to catch my eye! I strolled the length of Market Street to see what I might buy! And I bought...apples, books..." Each picture in this imaginative alphabet book is a person, created with the item named. For example, the letter *A* is a person made with apples.

Follow up a reading of this favorite alphabet book by gathering children in a circle and playing a Market Street game. Reread the first page of the story then invite a volunteer to say a word for *A*. Continue around the circle, letting each child tell what he or she might buy at the market for the next letter. Play until you reach the end of the alphabet. Record children's words, then let them each create a picture for a class Market Street book.

TIP

Write rhymes, chants, and fingerplays on a flip chart and let children take turns choosing one to chant or sing each day. If you have a daily class meeting, this might be a good time for this activity.

Where to Learn More

Build your class collection of chants, songs, action rhymes, riddles, and tongue twisters with *Juba This and Juba That*, selected by Virginia A. Tashjian (Little, Brown, 1995).

Letter Collage

A is for *apple, ant, art, Abraham Lincoln, alphabet, acorn, airplane, astronaut* … encouraging children to make connections between words (such as the first letter/beginning sound) builds reading and writing skills. Print large block letters on heavy-weight paper and tack them up around the room. Let children fill them in by pasting on pictures of things whose names start with each letter. You can send this activity home, too, giving children cards on which you've printed a block letter for the first letter of their names. They can work with their families to find and paste pictures that go with the letter.

BUILDING ON BOOKS

The Z Was Zapped: A Play in Twenty-Six Acts

by Chris Van Allsburg
(Houghton Mifflin, 1987)

This story is written in very brief acts—one for each letter.

"Act 1 The A... was an Avalanche

The B...was badly bitten..."

Alliteration reinforces sound-letter associations in this book. Read a few pages to give children the idea. Then read only the start of each sentence (*The C was* ...) and let children guess what comes next. Follow up by performing this little play. Give each child a letter, and let them take turns reading their lines aloud, using gestures and expressions to add to the performance.

ABC Hop

Turn a corner of your classroom into a game board. Write letters of the alphabet on 10-inch-square cards. You may want to make extra vowels. Laminate and tape to the floor, leaving a few inches between cards. Invite children to help make up games to play. For example, they might play in pairs, with one child calling out letters for the other to hop to, and then switching places. Or, one child can call out letters to spell a simple word, while the other child hops on the letters and tells what they spell. Children will have fun visiting on their own, too, hopping on letters and simply saying their names or using them to spell words of their own.

Bean Bag Letter Toss

This bean bag toss game invites children to show what they know about letters and sounds. Play a cooperative version so that children can ask one another for assistance if they wish.

☀ Set up the game by drawing eight to twelve large circles (at least eight inches) on a sheet of craft paper. You can create a pyramid shape with the circles or set them up in rows. Inside each circle write a different target letter (or initial blend). Tape the game board to the floor.

☀ Make bean bags by filling zip-close sandwich bags with dried beans.

☀ Let children take turns tossing a bean bag on the game board. Have them say the letter on the space that the bean bag lands on and call out a word that starts with the sound that letter makes. Continue playing until each child has at least one turn.

For a variation, let children piggyback on one another's words, building a sentence with words for the letters they land on. For example, if the first child lands on *A*, he or she might say *Annie*. The second child tosses a bean bag and says a word that both starts with the letter on the space and adds to the sentence beginning. If that letter is *L*, for example, he or she might add the word *likes*. The next child then adds to *Annie likes* with a word that starts with the letter he or she lands on. For example, if that letter is *M*, he or she might add *marshmallows*, making the sentence *Annie likes marshmallows*.

ABC Circus Train

ABC Circus Train

The letter _____ is dandy.

When I want to spell _____

It comes in very handy!

Name _____

Irresistible ABCs Scholastic Professional Books

ABC Circus Train

The letter _____ is dandy.

When I want to spell _____

It comes in very handy!

Name _____

Name _____ Date _____

Miss Mary Mack

Miss Mary Mack, Mack, Mack
All dressed in black, black, black
With silver buttons, buttons, buttons
All down her back, back, back...

She asked her mother, mother, mother
For 50 cents, cents, cents
To see the elephants, elephants, elephants
Jump over the fence, fence, fence.

They jumped so high, high, high
They reached the sky, sky, sky
And they didn't come back, back, back
'Til the 4th of July, ly, ly!

Clapping Pattern

1. Cross arms over chest.
2. Clap thighs.
3. Clap own hands.
4. Partners clap right hands.
5. Clap own hands.
6. Partners clap left hands.
7. Clap own hands.
8. Partners clap right hands.
9. Repeat 1–8.

Building on Letters and Words

Ring Around My Words

As students move from learning the ABCs to putting letters together to read and write words, make personalized word rings that put words that are important to children at their fingertips. Students can add a word a day (or every other day), and by the end of the year, they'll have a very special collection of words.

❂ Set up for this ongoing activity by prepunching a hole on the side or top of a supply of cards. You'll also need an O-ring for each child.

❂ Meet individually with each child for a few minutes. Slip a blank card on the O-ring and let the child write his or her name on it (or write the name for the child). Look at the name together. Notice features of the letters, such as shape.

❂ Ask the child to tell you another word that is important to him or her. This might be a pet's name, a favorite toy, and so on. Print this word on a second index card and slip it on the O-ring. Again, look at features of the letters together. Have the child illustrate the word on the card.

❂ Repeat the activity every day or two, reviewing words with children and adding and illustrating new words.

Encourage children to share their words with one another. They'll be excited and proud to watch their word rings—and their reading ability—grow.

Mary Beth Spann
Education Consultant
Shoreham Elementary School
Shoreham, New York

A Room for Writing

Encourage writing—from children's first explorations with letters to sentences and paragraphs—with a classroom that puts a wide assortment of writer's tools in easy access.

✸ Stock a writing center with all sorts of stationery, pens, pencils, and markers.

✸ Make class stationery with a computer program such as *ClarisWorks*.

✸ Place cardboard, craft sticks, and tape at the block center. Children can use the materials to make signs for structures they build. (Clay makes a sturdy sign base.)

✸ Provide labels and markers. Invite children to label the room.

✸ Nametags are always fun for children to make and wear. They can make their own or one for a friend.

✸ Include small memo pads at a play shopping center for making lists, receipts, and so on.

✸ Clip blank paper to clipboards. Hang them up around the room. Students will find a way to use them.

✸ Sentence strips, chart paper, and blank cards are just a few of the other writing supplies that will inspire children to write often and for many reasons.

BUILDING ON BOOKS

Alphabet Riddles

by Susan Joyce
(Peel Productions, 1998)

"I start with an A and end with a T. You also could say I end with a Z. I'm the symbols you use to write words you choose. What in the world can I possibly be?" Rhyming riddles introduce each letter of the alphabet. Use them as a model for writing class alphabet riddles. Write some together for a neighboring class to solve. Let children team up to write more to share.

Read and Write the Room

Simple props inspire children to learn more about letters in the print around their classroom.

Read the Wall: Provide nonprescription "reading glasses" and dowels made to look like pencils. Let students put on the glasses and take the "pencil" around the

"tip me over, and pour me out!"

room, pointing to and reading letters and words they see (labels, pocket charts, sentence strips, name tags, big books, and so on). Other fun props include a magic word wand. (Cut out the mesh center of a fly swatter and add lots of curly ribbon and glitter.)

Write the Wall: Decorate clipboards (paint them, add glitter borders, tie curly ribbon on the top) and provide assorted writing instruments. Let children walk around the room with clipboards in hand, using environmental print as inspiration and an aid for writing. (For example, beginning writers might copy words they see or use them in stories.)

Elaine Magud
Joshua Cowell School
Manteca, California

First-Grade Fast Words

Words such as *I*, *the*, *and*, and *it* are just a few of the many frequently used words in children's reading and writing. A display of "fast words" makes it easy for your students to spell these words correctly in their writing. To make the display, tack up several large sheets of craft paper. Divide the paper into 26 squares, one for each letter. Label the squares, and print the words that are part of your students' "high-frequency" word list under the appropriate letters. Add new "fast words" that you introduce throughout the year. You may also wish to make a "fast words" list for each child to clip inside a notebook or journal.

Jim Henry
Lomond Elementary School
Shaker Heights, Ohio

Fingers Spell Words

As children learn the written letters of the alphabet, you may also want to introduce them to the American Sign Language handshapes for each letter. Give each child a copy of page 43, which pictures each handshape, along with the written letter. Invite them to practice signing letters to become more familiar with this form of communication. Then try any of the following activities to do more.

☀ Line up children for a special performance of the alphabet song. Assign each child a letter to sign. As you sing the song, have children sign it! (Arrange children in alphabetical order based on the letters they are signing.)

☀ Invite a volunteer to come to the front of the group and sign any classmate's name. This child then comes up and signs another child's name. Continue until all children have had a chance to see their names signed and sign a classmate's name.

☀ Make copies of the handshapes on page 43. Cut out the

BUILDING ON BOOKS

The Handmade Alphabet
by Laura Rankin
(Scholastic, 1993)

Each page of this Reading Rainbow book shows a handshape for the manual alphabet, the corresponding letter of the written alphabet, and a softly rendered image. There are bubbles for *B*. *C* is a lovely tea cup. Icicles hang down on the page for I. Ribbon encircles the handshape for *R*. Introduce the manual alphabet to children with this book, inviting them to make the handshapes they see. *A Sign Language Alphabet: Handsigns* by Kathleen Fain (Scholastic, 1993) contains additional information about finger spelling. Share the pages of this book, then let students try finger spelling the name of the animal pictured for each letter of the alphabet. (See Fingers Spell Words, left, for more activities.)

handshapes (snip off the written form of the letter on each, as well as the picture) and use them to spell a secret message each day. Let children write the message in the written alphabet on slips of paper and put them in a box. At the end of the day, reveal the message.

☀ Take five or 10 minutes out of the day for communicating with the manual alphabet. Children can visit in small groups or with partners. The only rule is manual alphabet only.

Roll It, Say It, Spell It

Use the pattern on page 44 to make letter cubes. (See directions below.) Write different letters on the cubes, making sure to include a few vowels on each. Children can play many games with these letter cubes. Some suggestions follow, but be sure to invite your students to share their ideas, too.

☀ Roll the cube. Say a word that starts with that letter.

☀ Roll a cube five times (or some other number). What word can you make with the letters (some or all)?

☀ Roll a cube 50 times. Graph the letters as they are rolled. What letter comes out on top?

☀ Play in a small group, with each player rolling a cube. What word or words can you make together with the letters that are rolled?

1. Fold down all seven tabs along dotted rules.

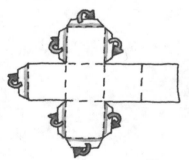

2. Fold down remaining dotted lines.

3. apply glue to out-facing surface of each tab.

4. Attach each tab to back surfaces of numbered squares.

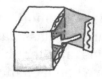

Stamp That Word

Stock a work table or center with a stack of one-inch grid paper (see page 45), alphabet stamps, and colorful ink pads. Provide word families to copy, a class list for learning names, sentence strips on which you've written words or sentences, and so on. Have children stamp what they see on the paper, one letter per space. This is a fun way to practice the week's spelling words, words from a thematic unit, and so on.

> Elaine Magud
> Joshua Cowell School
> Manteca, California

Scrambled Letter Sequencing Game

This game invites children to unscramble and sequence letters to make words. Copy the game pieces on page 46. Cut out the strips and tape A to B. Cut out the letter squares. Write a letter on each square to spell a six- or seven-letter word. You might choose words from a spelling list, students' names, characters from books, or words from theme units.

Let students play in pairs, placing the mixed-up letter cards on the strip to begin. (Empty spaces are okay.) Have students take turns moving the letter squares to sequence them and spell a word. Each player can move one card per turn, jumping over another card (into an empty space only) or sliding to an adjacent empty space.

> Mary Rosenberg
> Kratt Elementary School
> Fresno, California

You may opt to give some students an extra sentence strip on which you've written the letters in order. They can then use the strip as reference to move letters into position. Other students may be able to work without this extra help.

Hidden Words

Children love to find hidden words in their names. Write each child's name (first and/or last) on a sentence strip, leaving plenty of room between letters. Cut apart the letters and place in a recloseable sandwich bag. Give each child his or her letters. Let children experiment with the letters, arranging them to make words.

> Monica Lubic
> Charlotte Central School
> Charlotte, Vermont

TIP

This activity is easy to share at home, too. Just clip a note to each bag, inviting families to look for words together and list them on a piece of paper. Have children share their findings in class.

Name-a-Day

These name-a-day activities will keep your students learning about letters all year. Write each child's name on a slip of paper. Have one child draw a slip from the box. Choose from the following activities to help children learn more.

* Invite students to interview the child to discover his or her likes and dislikes, favorite foods, pets, brothers and sisters, and so on.

* Write the child's name on a sentence strip while classmates watch. Point out the use of a capital letter at the beginning and lowercase letters for the rest of the letters.

* Write the name again on a sentence strip and cut apart the letters. Let children spell the name by organizing the letters in the proper order in a pocket chart.

* Have each child write the Name-a-Day child's name in large letters at the top of a sheet of paper. Ask children to add information they know about the child by drawing pictures or writing words. Staple all of these pages together to make a book for that child.

* At the end of the day, pack up the pocket chart letters and book for the child to bring home. Children will look forward to sharing the materials with their families— reading the book with them and putting the pocket chart letters together.

> Charlotte Sassman
> Alice Carlson Applied Learning Center
> Fort Worth, Texas

My Name and More! Mini-Book

The first time a child reads or writes his or her name is a memorable one. Making associations between the sounds and letters in a name and other words helps a child learn to read and spell new words. Make mini-books that invite children to make these connections. Cut copy paper in half or quarters and staple a stack of five to ten sheets to make a book. Let children write their first names on the cover. Have them write words that start with the same sound on each additional page. Children can illustrate their books then read them aloud.

Peg Arcadi
Homeschool
Trumansburg, New York

Stand-Up Sentences

After sharing a predictable book or poem (see Where to Learn More, page 40, for suggestions), copy the text from about two pages on index cards. Make a card for each word and punctuation mark on the pages. Pass out the words and punctuation marks and let children examine them. Begin to read the selected text, asking children to follow along as you point to the words. When children find words and punctuation marks that match theirs, have them come to the front of the group. Encourage children to pay close attention to the first letter/sound of each word. This will help beginning readers recognize their words. Stop after each sentence to let children arrange themselves in the order of the words on the page. Children who are not part of a particular sentence can read the words from the cards.

Charlotte Sassman
Alice Carlson Applied Learning Center
Fort Worth, Texas

Children who are not writing independently may dictate the words for you to write down. Or, you can write the words on a separate sheet of paper and children can copy them into their books.

39

Where to Learn More

Getting the Most from Predictable Books by Michael Opitz (Scholastic Professional Books, 1995) contains strategies and activities for teaching with more than 75 predictable books. A sampling of titles follows.

☀ *Bringing the Rain to Kapiti Plain* Verna Aardema (Scholastic, 1991)

☀ *Dogs Don't Wear Sneakers* by Laura Joffe Numeroff (Simon & Schuster, 1993)

☀ *Is Your Mama a Llama?* by Deborah Guarino (Scholastic, 1989)

☀ *One Monday Morning* by Uri Shulevitz (Scribner, 1967)

☀ *When It Comes to Bugs* by Aileen Fisher (HarperCollins, 1986)

Add-a-Letter Word Building Game

Play a word-building game using phonograms to help students learn to recognize chunks and use them to read and write new words. Make copies of the gameboard on page 47 for each pair of students. Laminate for durability if desired. Give each set of students a gameboard, two pennies, and game markers. To play, have children take turns shaking and "rolling" the pennies: two heads = move one space; two tails = move two spaces; one head, one tail = move three spaces. When children land on a space, have them add a letter to the beginning of the letters on the space to make a word. Have children record the words they make. Children can play until each child reaches the end. Invite children to read aloud the words they built. They can play again and again, each time using the familiar phonograms to create new words!

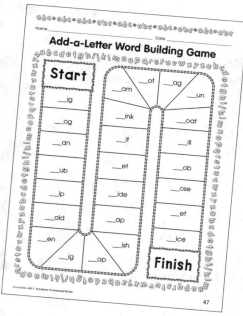

Copy the gameboard for students to play at home with their families. Include a note explaining how to play.

BUILDING ON BOOKS

A My Name Is Alice
by Jane Byer
(Dial, 1984)

You might remember bouncing a ball to this chant as a child. Here it's redone as an alphabet book. Let children add their own verses based on their names (or any name they'd like to substitute). Invite them to bounce a ball as they share their rhymes for the full effect.

Celebrating and Sharing

Learning the letters of the alphabet, the sounds each one makes, and the words they can form by putting letters together is one of the most exciting accomplishments for young children. Celebrate children's successes in this process by giving them an audience with which to share their writing. Even children who are in the earliest stages of putting letters together to form words have important stories to share.

One of the ways to provide an audience is to have children read their work aloud. This approach doubles as a way to develop speaking skills. Introduce oration skills early to give young children plenty of time to prepare for later standardized tests that cover this area, also to give them a strong foundation for the times in school and beyond that call for speaking skills. Children whose writing resembles scribbles on a page can share just as children who are writing words, sentences, and paragraphs. Tips for strengthening speaking skills follow.

☀ Children who are uncomfortable sharing with the whole class can share with a partner or small group.

☀ Give children time to practice reading aloud. They can take turns standing in the front of the room and talking to children in the back. Have them adjust their volume until they can be heard comfortably.

☀ When you read aloud to children, vary your expression and tone. Children will pick up on this and apply it more easily when they read aloud.

> Monica Lubic
> Charlotte Central School
> Charlotte, Vermont

Flash Card Line Up

Write children's names on flash cards. Give each child his or her name card. Have children work together to line up in alphabetical order. Discuss children's strategies for accomplishing the task, including what they need to do when two children's names start with the same letter. Let children take turns reading the names in alphabetical order. Talk about new strategies for lining up by name cards and let them try again!

> Natalie Vaughan
> Phoenix School
> Encinitas, California

TIP

For a more challenging version of this line-up game, pass out the cards randomly. Have the child who is holding the name card that comes first in alphabetical order find that child and trade cards. The child with the name that comes first goes to the front of the line. The child holding the card that comes next gives it to the correct child who then takes the second place in line. This continues until every child is in alphabetical order.

We're Word Builders!

Play a matching game to help children see how they can put letters together to make words.

☀ Make a set of game cards by writing word parts on index cards. Make sure that for every part, there is a matching part so that when combined, they will form a word.

☀ Give each child a game card. Have children walk about the room, looking for a classmate to combine cards with and build a word.

☀ When everyone has a match, let students share their words.

☀ Play again, mixing up the cards (or using a new set) and letting children build new words.

"Go Fish" Rhyming Game

This game helps children build early reading skills with word families. As they begin to recognize the sounds that some groups of letters make (phonograms) they can more quickly read and write new words. It's played like the traditional game of Go Fish, with children looking for rhyming word pairs rather than number matches. To prepare the game, make several copies of the card templates on page 48. Cut apart the cards. Select two words from each word family you want to focus on and print each on a card. (See suggestions below.) Make about 36 cards—or 18 sets— in all. Have children play in groups of two to three, following these steps.

☀ Deal seven cards to each player. Place remaining cards face down in the middle.

☀ Take turns asking another player for a card. If this child has the card, he or she gives it to the other child, who then places the matching cards down face up and reads them aloud. If the child does not have the card in question, he or she says "Go Fish" and the player selects a card from the center.

☀ Play continues until children match all of their cards.

Add a playful touch to your word-building game by playing music while children find their matches.

You can also make sets of three rhyming word cards and challenge children to collect all three to make a set. Or, have children play to get either two or three matching cards, with other players being allowed to add matching cards to any set of two that another player puts down.

Suggested rhyming word pairs for Go Fish follow:

Long -a: cake, lake; face, race

Long -e: bee, tree; feet, meet

Long -i: bike, hike; mice, nice

Long -o: rose, nose; no, go

Short -a: bat, cat; cap, nap

Short -e: jet, pet; bell, tell

Short -i: pig, big; fish, dish

Short -o: hop, pop; rock, sock

Short -u: cup, pup; sun, fun

Name _____ Date _____

Fingers Spell Words

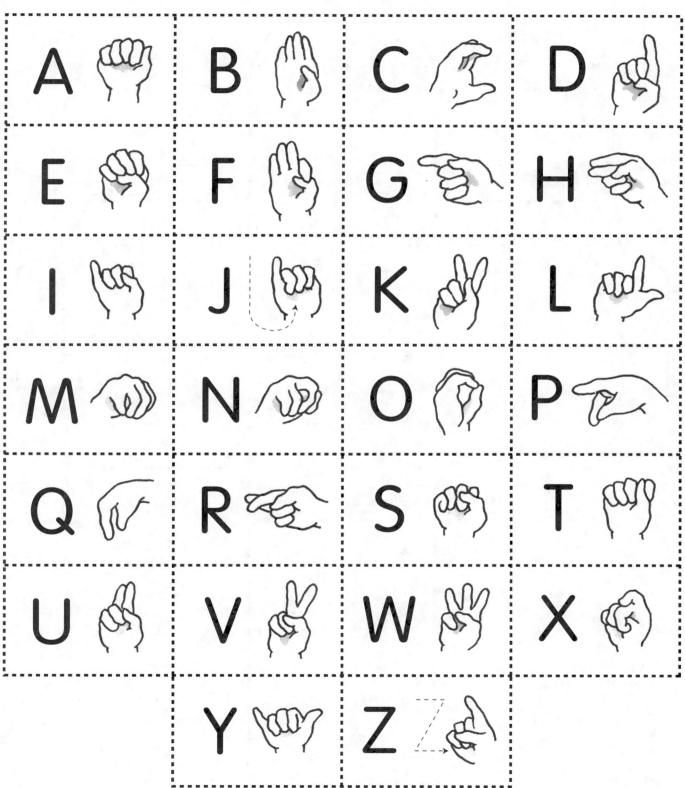

Letter Cubes

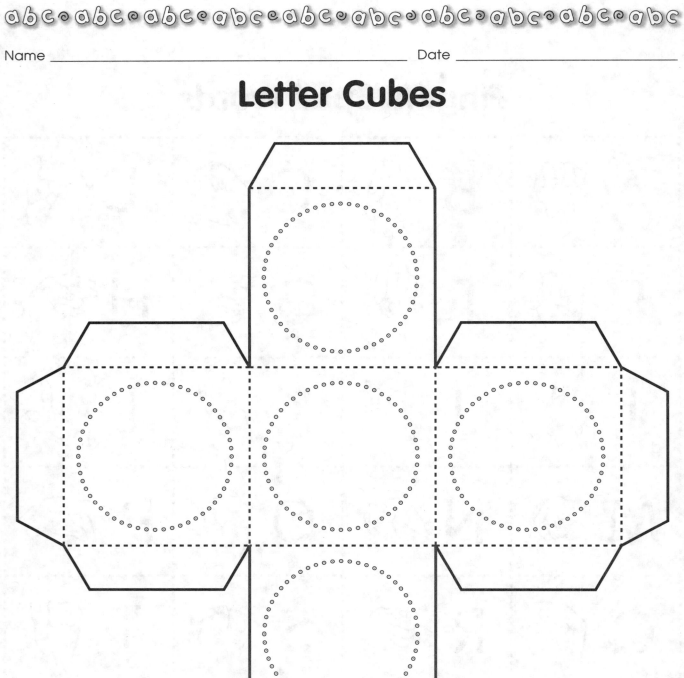

Name _____ Date _____

Stamp That Word

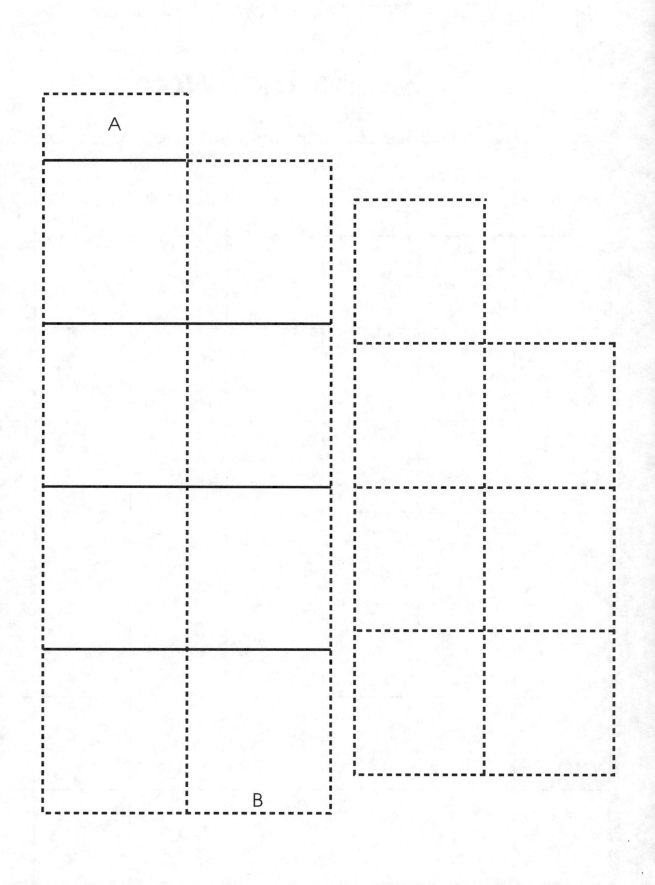

A

B

46

Name _____ Date _____

Add-a-Letter Word Building Game

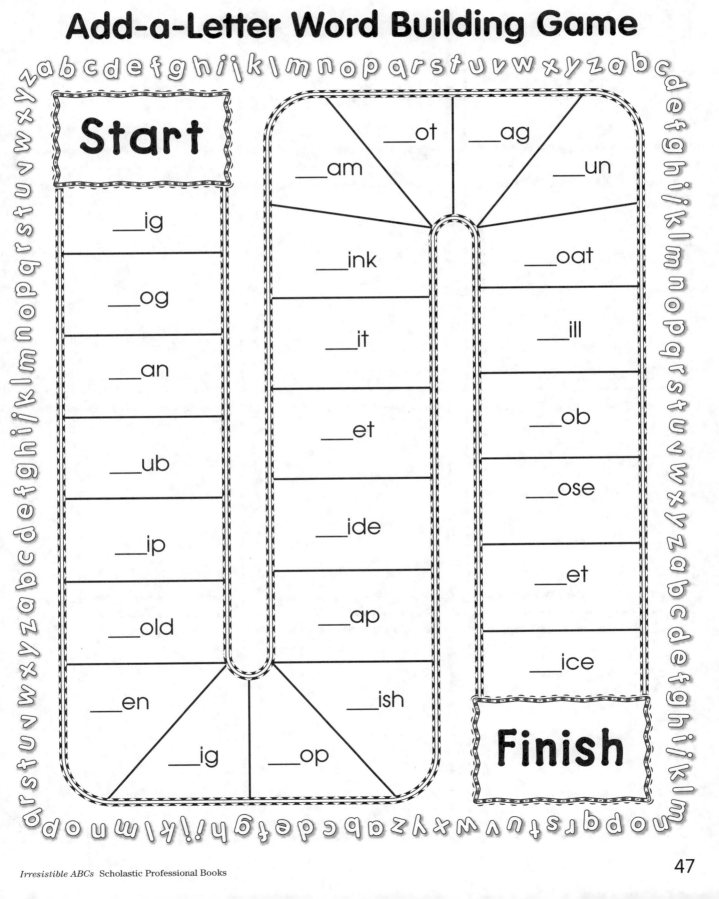

abcdefghijklmnopqrstuvwxyzabcdefghijklmnopqrstuvwxyzabcdefghijklmnopqrstuvwxyz

Start

___ig

___og

___an

___ub

___ip

___old

___en

___ig

___ot

___am

___ink

___it

___et

___ide

___ap

___ish

___op

___ag

___un

___oat

___ill

___ob

___ose

___et

___ice

Finish

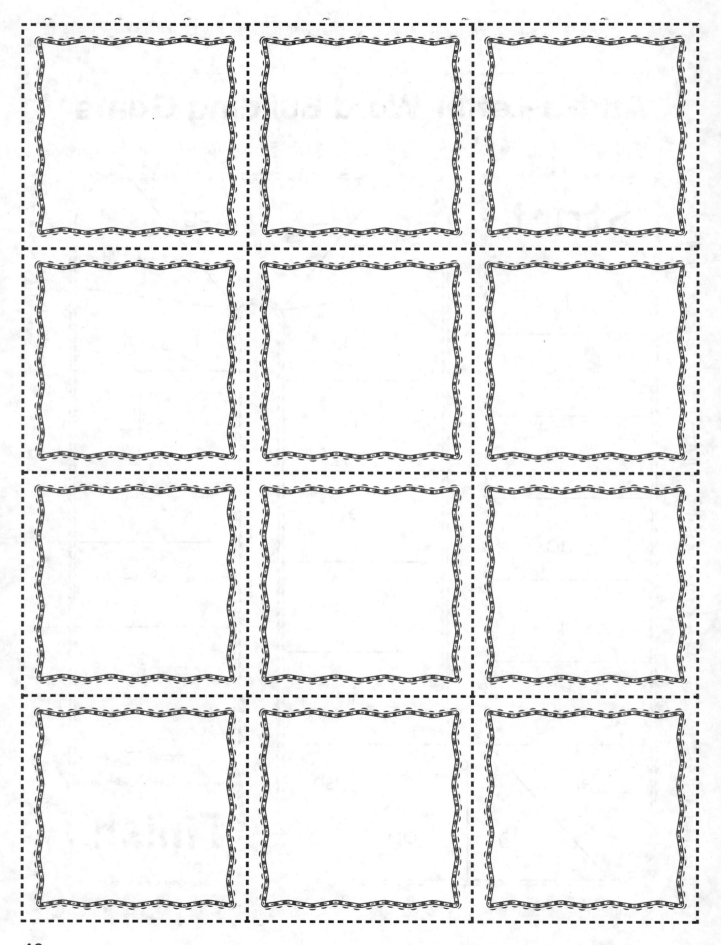

48